BELGRADE

21 THINGS TO DO IN 7 DAYS

1. Kalemegdan Fortress

Kalemegdan Fortress, often regarded as the heart of Belgrade, is a historic gem offering an incredible journey through time. This ancient fortress is perched atop a cliff, where the Sava and Danube rivers meet, providing breathtaking panoramic views of the city.

Kalemegdan Fortress is conveniently located in the city center, making it easily accessible on foot from many parts of Belgrade. Alternatively, you can take a tram, bus, or taxi to reach the fortress. The address is Kalemegdan, Belgrade 11000, Serbia.

Entrance to the Kalemegdan Fortress is generally free. However, you may need to pay a nominal fee (around 200 Serbian dinars) to enter the Military Museum located within the fortress, which houses a remarkable collection of artifacts and historical exhibits.

Once inside the fortress, you'll find a vast, sprawling complex to explore. Stroll along the ancient walls, visit the multiple museums, and take in the breathtaking views from various vantage points. The clock tower, Pobednik Monument, and Sahat Kula (The Clock Gate) are must-see highlights. Don't forget to explore the beautiful park that surrounds the fortress.

Exploring Kalemegdan Fortress can take anywhere from 1 to 3 hours, depending on your level of interest and the time you spend enjoying the views and attractions.

Consider visiting in the late afternoon to catch a stunning sunset over the confluence of the rivers.

Wear comfortable shoes for walking, as the terrain can be uneven.

Guided tours are available for a more in-depth understanding of the fortress's history.

Bring some water and snacks, as there aren't many refreshment options within the fortress.

Kalemegdan Fortress is a must-visit in Belgrade, offering a rich blend of history, culture, and stunning vistas, making it a memorable experience for any traveler.

2. Skadarlija (Bohemian Quarter)

Skadarlija is the epitome of bohemian charm in Belgrade. Nestled in the heart of the city, this cobblestone street is lined with picturesque cafes, taverns, and art galleries. It's a place where history, culture, and great food come together to create an unforgettable experience.

Skadarlija is situated in the Stari Grad (Old Town) district, near the city center. You can easily reach it on foot from key locations like Republic Square or Kalemegdan Fortress. Alternatively, you can take a taxi or public transportation.

There's no entrance fee to access Skadarlija. You're free to wander along the charming street without any cost. However, you'll need to pay for the food, drinks, and entertainment you choose to enjoy at the various venues.

Skadarlija's main attractions are its traditional restaurants, where you can savor authentic Serbian cuisine and listen to live music. Don't miss out on trying local specialties like ćevapi, sarma, and rakija. You can also explore art shops, galleries, and vintage stores in the area. The atmosphere in the evening is particularly lively, with live bands and performances adding to the Bohemian spirit.

The amount of time spent in Skadarlija can vary, but most visitors find a few hours to be sufficient to enjoy a meal, listen to live music, and explore the charming surroundings. If you're a fan of Serbian cuisine and music, you may wish to stay longer into the evening.

Skadarlija can get crowded in the evenings, so making a reservation at a restaurant is a good idea.

Keep in mind that some places may have cover charges for live music, so inquire about this before entering.

Skadarlija offers a unique and nostalgic experience, transporting visitors to a bygone era of art, culture, and hearty Serbian feasts. It's an essential stop for anyone looking to capture the essence of Belgrade's bohemian spirit.

3. Republic Square

Republic Square, or Trg Republike in Serbian, stands as the central square in Belgrade, and it's a bustling hub of cultural, historical, and architectural significance. This square is where Belgrade's past and present converge, offering a vibrant mix of attractions.

Republic Square is located at the very heart of Belgrade, making it accessible by foot from most parts of the city center. If you're coming from a little farther, you can use public transportation, including trams and buses. It's also a well-known point of reference for taxi drivers.

Entrance to Republic Square is entirely free. However, you may wish to budget for any attractions or activities you choose to participate in while you're in the area.

Republic Square is home to several prominent landmarks, including the National Museum, the National Theatre, and the statue of Prince Mihailo on a horse. Visit the National Museum to explore the extensive art and historical collections. Catch a performance or a ballet at the National Theatre. Stroll around the square and enjoy the lively atmosphere, or have a coffee at one of the many cafes. The square is particularly charming in the evening when it's illuminated.

The duration of your visit to Republic Square can vary depending on your interests. Exploring the National Museum may take a few hours, while a casual stroll and coffee break could be completed in an hour or two.

Republic Square often hosts events, protests, and gatherings, so you might come across something unexpected during your visit.

Nearby, Knez Mihailova Street is a famous shopping and dining area, so consider exploring it after visiting the square.

Republic Square is not just a central point on the map, but a dynamic gathering place that encapsulates the spirit of Belgrade. Whether you're interested in art, history, or simply enjoying the city's pulse, a visit to Republic Square is a must.

4. St. Sava Temple

The St. Sava Temple, also known as Hram Svetog Save, is a monumental Orthodox Christian cathedral and a symbol of faith and identity for the people of Belgrade and Serbia. Situated in the Vračar district, it is one of the largest Orthodox churches in the world, and its gleaming white domes can be seen from afar.

The St. Sava Temple is centrally located and can be easily reached from various parts of Belgrade. You can take a taxi, public transportation (buses or trams), or simply walk from the city center. The address is Karadorđeva Street, Belgrade 11000, Serbia.

Entrance to the temple is typically free, and visitors are welcome to enter and explore. However, there may be small fees for certain activities, like visiting the crypt or the church's galleries.

The main attraction is the stunning interior of the cathedral, adorned with intricate mosaics and rich religious artwork. Take the time to admire the magnificent central dome and the massive chandelier, one of the largest in the world. If you're interested in history, consider visiting the crypt, which houses an exhibition about the church's construction. The peaceful park surrounding the temple is an excellent place for a leisurely stroll or a moment of reflection.

Visiting the St. Sava Temple can take around 1 to 2 hours, depending on how much time you spend admiring the interior and exploring the surrounding area.

Dress modestly and respectfully, as it is an active place of worship.

Photography is generally allowed, but be discreet and respectful of the worshippers.

The temple can be crowded on weekends and during religious holidays, so plan your visit accordingly for a quieter experience.

The St. Sava Temple is a place of spiritual and architectural significance, and it offers a serene and contemplative experience. Whether you're interested in religion, history, or simply enjoying beautiful art and architecture, this iconic landmark is worth a visit while in Belgrade.

5. Nikola Tesla Museum

The Nikola Tesla Museum in Belgrade is a captivating homage to one of the world's greatest inventors, Nikola Tesla. The museum is dedicated to his life and work, showcasing an impressive collection of his inventions and innovations that forever changed the world of electricity and technology.

The Nikola Tesla Museum is conveniently located in the city center, near other popular attractions. It's easily accessible by foot, public transportation (buses and trams), or taxi. The museum's address is Krunska 51, Belgrade 11000, Serbia.

The approximate ticket price for adults is around 500 Serbian dinars, with reduced prices for students, children, and groups. The admission fee includes a guided tour of the museum.

Explore the life and work of Nikola Tesla through a guided tour of the museum's exhibits. You'll have the opportunity to see Tesla's personal effects, scientific instruments, and working models of his inventions. The highlight of the tour is the Tesla coil demonstration, which provides a spectacular display of electricity.

Visiting the Nikola Tesla Museum typically takes around 1 to 1.5 hours, including the guided tour. The tour guide will provide valuable insights into Tesla's groundbreaking work.

The museum is closed on Mondays, so plan your visit accordingly.

Guided tours are available in various languages, so check the schedule and availability.

Photography is allowed inside the museum, but ask your guide for specific guidelines.

The museum's gift shop offers a selection of books and souvenirs related to Nikola Tesla.

A visit to the Nikola Tesla Museum is an enlightening journey into the life and inventions of a true visionary. Whether you're a history buff, a technology enthusiast, or simply curious about the world-changing discoveries of Tesla, this museum offers a fascinating experience that's both educational and inspiring.

6. Belgrade Zoo

The Belgrade Zoo, known as Beo Zoo Vrt in Serbian, is a wonderful oasis in the heart of the city, offering a diverse collection of animals and a tranquil escape from the urban bustle. It's an ideal destination for nature and animal lovers of all ages.

The Belgrade Zoo is located in Kalemegdan Park, adjacent to the Kalemegdan Fortress and near the confluence of the Sava and Danube rivers. You can easily reach it by foot, taxi, or public transportation, such as trams and buses. The address is Kalemegdan, Mali Kalemegdan, Belgrade 11000, Serbia.

The approximate ticket price for adults is around 500 Serbian dinars, with reduced fees for children, students, and seniors. It's one of the more affordable attractions in Belgrade. Your admission supports the care of the animals and the maintenance of the zoo.

Stroll through the zoo's well-maintained pathways to view a wide array of animals, including big cats, primates, exotic birds, and various species from around the world. Don't miss the opportunity to visit the zoo's aquarium, which houses an impressive selection of aquatic creatures. The zoo also offers educational programs, and it's an excellent place for family outings and picnics.

Exploring the Belgrade Zoo typically takes around 2 to 3 hours, depending on your level of interest and the pace of your visit.

The zoo is open year-round, but it's especially enjoyable during the spring and early summer when the weather is pleasant.

The zoo's staff is dedicated to conservation and animal welfare. Consider supporting their efforts through donations or by adopting an animal.

The Belgrade Zoo offers a unique opportunity to connect with wildlife in the heart of the city. It's an educational and enjoyable experience, perfect for families and nature enthusiasts, and it provides a refreshing break from the urban surroundings of Belgrade.

7. Ada Ciganlija (Lake Ada)

Ada Ciganlija, often referred to as "Belgrade's Sea," is a beautiful artificial lake and river island located in the Sava River, just a stone's throw away from the city center. It's a popular recreational spot, offering a wide range of outdoor activities and natural beauty.

Ada Ciganlija is easily accessible from the city center, and there are several ways to get there. You can take a taxi, use public transportation (bus lines 52, 53, or 56), or simply stroll or bike along the Ada Bridge. The address is Ada Ciganlija, Belgrade 11000, Serbia.

Entrance to Ada Ciganlija is generally free. However, you may need to pay for parking, water sports, and certain activities like renting bikes, paddleboats, or sunbeds.

The options at Ada Ciganlija are diverse. You can swim in the lake, relax on the beach, or rent paddleboats or kayaks for water fun. The island is also a popular spot for jogging, cycling, and rollerblading, with a 7-kilometer-long "skejt" track. Numerous cafes, restaurants, and bars cater to different tastes, making it a fantastic place for a meal or a refreshing drink.

The amount of time spent at Ada Ciganlija varies based on your interests and activities. You can enjoy a leisurely day at the beach, have a picnic, or engage in sports and recreational pursuits. A half-day to a full day is typical for most visitors.

Bring sunscreen and swimwear during the summer months, as the lake offers a pleasant escape from the heat.

Be cautious with personal belongings, especially on crowded days.

Check the operating hours of any specific activities you plan to enjoy, as they may vary.

The island hosts various events, concerts, and festivals during the year, so keep an eye out for any exciting happenings during your visit.

Ada Ciganlija is a serene haven offering an abundance of leisure and outdoor activities. Whether you're seeking relaxation, adventure, or a mix of both, this beautiful urban oasis provides the ideal escape from Belgrade's bustling city life.

8. House of Flowers (Josip Broz Tito's Mausoleum)

The House of Flowers, or Kuća Cveća in Serbian, is a unique and historically significant museum located in Belgrade. This mausoleum is the final resting place of Josip Broz Tito, Yugoslavia's former leader. It offers a captivating glimpse into his life and the legacy of the once-unified country.

The House of Flowers is situated in the Dedinje district, approximately 5 kilometers from Belgrade's city center. You can easily reach it by taxi or public transportation. Bus lines 27 and 27E run to the nearby bus stop, and from there, it's a short walk to the museum. The address is Botićeva 6, Belgrade 11040, Serbia.

The approximate ticket price for adults is around 400 Serbian dinars, with reduced fees for students, children, and seniors. The admission includes access to both the House of Flowers and the Museum 25th of May, which houses an extensive collection of Tito-related artifacts.

The House of Flowers is a place of historical significance, offering visitors a glimpse into Tito's life, his state funerals, and the Yugoslav era. You can view Tito's tomb, personal items, and the floral displays he received. The museum also houses gifts from foreign dignitaries and showcases photographs and documents of the time.

Exploring the House of Flowers and the Museum 25th of May typically takes around 1 to 1.5 hours, depending on your interest in history and your pace.

Photography inside the mausoleum is generally not allowed, so please respect this rule.

The museum can get crowded during holidays or special events, so plan your visit accordingly for a more tranquil experience.

The House of Flowers offers a unique and thought-provoking experience for those interested in Yugoslav history and Tito's legacy. It provides a glimpse into the life and times of an influential leader and a bygone era of Southeastern European history.

9. Museum of Yugoslav History

The Museum of Yugoslav History, located in Belgrade, offers a captivating journey through the history of Yugoslavia. This institution is dedicated to preserving the memory of the former multi-ethnic nation and its influential leaders, particularly Josip Broz Tito.

The museum is situated in the Dedinje district, near the House of Flowers and the White Palace. It is easily accessible by taxi, public transportation, or on foot. Bus lines 40, 41, and 59 will take you to the nearby bus stop. The address is Botićeva 6, Belgrade 11040, Serbia.

The approximate ticket price for adults is around 300 Serbian dinars, with reduced fees for students, children, and seniors. Your ticket provides access to the museum's permanent and temporary exhibitions.

The Museum of Yugoslav History houses a diverse collection of artifacts, photographs, and documents that showcase the political, cultural, and social history of Yugoslavia. Explore the life and times of Josip Broz Tito, the Yugoslav leader, and visit his mausoleum. You can also wander through the Memorial Park, where Tito's resting place is surrounded by a garden and sculptures.

Visiting the museum typically takes around 1 to 2 hours, depending on your level of interest in history and the amount of time you spend exploring the exhibitions and the Memorial Park.

The museum is closed on Mondays, so plan your visit accordingly.

Photography inside the mausoleum and the exhibits may be restricted, so please follow any guidelines provided by museum staff.

Guided tours are available and can offer deeper insights into the history of Yugoslavia and the life of Tito.

The Museum of Yugoslav History is an essential destination for history enthusiasts and anyone interested in understanding the complex and multifaceted history of Yugoslavia. It's a place to reflect on the legacy of Tito and the country that once united different ethnicities in a shared nation.

10. Kalenic Market

Kalenic Market, or Kalenićeva Pijaca in Serbian, is a bustling open-air market in Belgrade where locals and tourists alike can savor the flavors of Serbia. This vibrant market is an excellent place to discover fresh produce, artisanal products, and experience authentic Serbian cuisine.

Kalenic Market is conveniently located in the Vračar district, near the city center. It's easily accessible on foot or by public transportation, with numerous tram and bus lines serving the area. The address is Kalenićeva, Vračar, Belgrade 11000, Serbia.

Entrance to Kalenic Market is entirely free. You're welcome to explore and savor the food and products without any cost.

Wander through the market's vibrant stalls and stands, which are brimming with fresh fruits, vegetables, cheeses, meats, baked goods, and more. Taste Serbian specialties like ćevapi, ajvar, and kajmak, or purchase locally sourced ingredients to enjoy later. The market is also an excellent place to interact with locals and experience the authentic food culture of Belgrade.

The amount of time spent at Kalenic Market can vary depending on your level of interest and whether you plan to enjoy a meal or simply browse. Most visitors find a couple of hours to be sufficient for a leisurely visit.

Kalenic Market is particularly lively in the morning, so it's a great spot to start your day.

Be prepared to pay in cash, as some vendors may not accept credit cards.

Explore the market's surrounding streets and discover charming cafes, restaurants, and shops.

Engage with local vendors, ask questions, and try some samples to fully appreciate the flavors and products on offer.

Kalenic Market is not only a culinary delight but also an opportunity to immerse yourself in the rich food culture of Belgrade. Whether you're a food enthusiast or simply looking for an authentic experience, the market offers a true taste of Serbia.

11. Church of Saint Mark

The Church of Saint Mark, or Crkva Svetog Marka in Serbian, is one of Belgrade's most iconic religious landmarks, known for its stunning architectural design and historical significance. This Serbian Orthodox church is located in the Tašmajdan Park area and offers a captivating blend of spirituality and artistry.

The Church of Saint Mark is situated in the Tašmajdan Park, close to the city center. You can easily reach it by walking or taking public transportation. Bus lines 31, 46, and 55, as well as trams 6, 7, and 12, provide convenient access. The address is Bulevar kralja Aleksandra 17, Belgrade 11000, Serbia.

Entrance to the church is generally free. However, if you wish to access the church's bell tower for panoramic views of the city, there may be a small fee, typically around 200 Serbian dinars.

Explore the remarkable architecture of the Church of Saint Mark, characterized by its beautiful frescoes and striking exterior. Admire the religious artwork, icons, and the serene interior. If you opt to pay a small fee, you can climb the bell tower for panoramic views of Belgrade, which is particularly stunning at sunset.

A visit to the Church of Saint Mark typically takes around 30 minutes to 1 hour, depending on the time spent exploring the interior and ascending the bell tower.

The church can get busy on religious holidays or during services, so it's best to plan your visit during quieter times.

Photography inside the church may be restricted, so please follow any guidelines provided by the church staff.

The Church of Saint Mark is a serene and historically significant place where you can admire impressive religious architecture and gain insight into the spiritual aspect of Belgrade. Whether you're interested in religious history, art, or simply seeking a peaceful atmosphere, this church provides a captivating experience.

12. Tašmajdan Park

Tašmajdan Park, nestled in the heart of Belgrade, is a tranquil urban oasis where nature, hi. and culture harmoniously coexist. This lush park offers respite from the city's hustle and bus and an array of activities for visitors to enjoy.

Tašmajdan Park is conveniently located in the city center, making it accessible on foot or via public transportation. Several bus and tram lines serve the area, and the park is close to notable landmarks like the Church of Saint Mark and the University of Belgrade. The address is Tašmajdan Park, Beograd 11000, Serbia.

Entrance to Tašmajdan Park is entirely free. Visitors are welcome to explore its verdant lawns, meandering paths, and cultural sites without any cost.

Wander through the park's picturesque gardens and enjoy a leisurely stroll. You can admire the monumental St. Mark's Church, a beautiful Serbian Orthodox church, or visit the Tašmajdan Sports and Recreation Center, which includes a swimming pool complex. The park also hosts various events and cultural activities, so it's a good idea to check for any happenings during your visit.

The duration of your visit to Tašmajdan Park can vary based on your interests and activities. A relaxed walk through the park and some leisurely exploration can take anywhere from 1 to 2 hours.

The park is an ideal spot for a picnic, so consider bringing some snacks or sandwiches.

Pay a visit to St. Mark's Church, an architectural gem with stunning frescoes and religious significance.

The park is known for its pleasant atmosphere in all seasons, from the blossoms of spring to the colorful foliage of autumn.

Tašmajdan Park provides a serene escape into nature within the bustling city center of Belgrade. It's a versatile destination suitable for relaxation, exploration, and cultural appreciation, and it's a popular choice for both locals and tourists seeking a refreshing break from urban life.

13. Avala Tower

The Avala Tower, or Avalski Toranj in Serbian, stands as an iconic symbol of Belgrade, offering visitors the chance to enjoy breathtaking panoramic views of the city and its surroundings. This telecommunications tower, rich in history, provides an exciting vantage point for exploring the Serbian capital.

Avala Tower is located on Mount Avala, which is approximately 16 kilometers from the city center. You can reach it by car, taxi, or public transportation, including bus lines 400, 401, or 402. The address is Omladinskih brigada 1, Belgrade 11000, Serbia.

The approximate ticket price for adults to access the observation deck is typically around 300 Serbian dinars, with reduced prices for students and children. The price may also include entrance to the nearby Monument to the Unknown Hero.

Ascend the tower's observation deck, which is situated at a height of 122 meters. From here, you can enjoy breathtaking panoramic views of Belgrade, the confluence of the Sava and Danube rivers, and the surrounding landscape. The tower also houses a café and a revolving restaurant where you can savor a meal or coffee while taking in the scenery.

A visit to Avala Tower usually takes around 1 to 2 hours, allowing you ample time to admire the views, relax at the café, and perhaps enjoy a meal.

The tower can be windy and chilly, so bring a light jacket or sweater, even in warm weather.

Be prepared for some waiting time at the elevator, especially on busy days.

The Monument to the Unknown Hero, which commemorates soldiers who died in World War I, is located nearby and is worth a visit in conjunction with Avala Tower.

Avala Tower provides an opportunity to see Belgrade from a whole new perspective. Whether you're a photography enthusiast, a nature lover, or simply looking for a unique experience, the tower offers a memorable outing with panoramic views that are second to none in the city.

14. Belgrade Museum of Contemporary Art

The Belgrade Museum of Contemporary Art, or Muzej savremene umetnosti in Serbian, is a cultural gem that showcases the works of contemporary Serbian and international artists. Located in a striking building, this museum offers visitors a glimpse into the vibrant world of modern art.

The museum is conveniently situated in the city center, near the confluence of the Sava and Danube rivers. You can easily reach it by walking or using public transportation. Bus lines 16, 84, and 704, as well as tram line 7, serve the area. The address is Usce 10, Belgrade 11000, Serbia.

The approximate ticket price for adults is around 300 Serbian dinars, with reduced prices for students, children, and seniors. The museum also offers free admission on Sundays, making it accessible to a broader audience.

Explore the museum's diverse collection of contemporary artworks, including paintings, sculptures, installations, and multimedia pieces. The exhibits often rotate, offering a fresh perspective on the world of modern art. Take your time to appreciate the creativity and innovation of both Serbian and international artists.

A visit to the Belgrade Museum of Contemporary Art typically takes around 1.5 to 2 hours, allowing you to enjoy the current exhibitions and engage with the art.

Check the museum's website or inquire about special exhibitions or events that may coincide with your visit.

Photography may be restricted in some areas, so please follow any guidelines provided by museum staff.

The Belgrade Museum of Contemporary Art is a testament to the city's vibrant and evolving art scene. Whether you're an art enthusiast, a creative spirit, or someone simply looking to experience the modern artistic landscape of Belgrade, this museum offers an enriching and inspiring cultural experience.

15. Danube River Cruises

Danube River Cruises in Belgrade offer a delightful way to experience the city from a unique perspective, as you glide along the majestic Danube River and take in the stunning landscapes. These cruises provide a serene and picturesque journey, showcasing Belgrade's riverside beauty.

Cruise embarkation points are usually along the Sava and Danube rivers, near popular locations such as Branko's Bridge and Ada Ciganlija. You can easily reach these points by taxi, public transportation, or even on foot, depending on your location in the city.

The ticket prices for Danube River Cruises vary depending on the type of cruise, duration, and inclusions. On average, a standard sightseeing cruise may cost between 500 to 1000 Serbian dinars per person. Some cruises offer dining options or guided tours for a higher price.

During the cruise, you'll have the opportunity to enjoy stunning panoramic views of Belgrade, including historic landmarks, iconic bridges, and beautiful riverbanks. Many cruises provide commentary in multiple languages, offering insights into the city's history and culture as you sail.

The duration of a Danube River Cruise can range from 1 to 2 hours for standard sightseeing cruises, while dining cruises and special events may last longer. The length of your cruise experience will depend on the type of tour you choose.

To secure your preferred cruise time and date, it's advisable to book in advance, especially during the busy tourist season.

Cruises are often available with live music, making for a more enjoyable and entertaining journey.

Danube River Cruises are a tranquil and memorable way to explore Belgrade's scenic riverside and experience the city's allure from a different angle. Whether you're a sightseeing enthusiast, a romantic traveler, or simply looking for a peaceful escape, a cruise along the Danube River offers a memorable and picturesque experience in the heart of Belgrade.

16. Museum of African Art

The Museum of African Arts, or Muzej Afričke Umetnosti in Serbian, is a hidden treasure in the heart of Belgrade. This unique institution is dedicated to celebrating the rich and diverse cultures of Africa, offering a captivating journey into the continent's artistic expressions.

The museum is located in the historic district of Dedinje, roughly 5 kilometers from the city center. You can easily reach it by taxi, public transportation, or a pleasant walk from central Belgrade. Bus lines 31 and 48, as well as tram line 3, serve the area. The address is Andre Nikolića 14, Belgrade 11000, Serbia.

The approximate ticket price for adults is around 300 Serbian dinars, with reduced fees for students, children, and seniors. The museum is known for its affordability, making it accessible to a wide range of visitors.

Explore the museum's diverse collection of African art, including sculptures, masks, textiles, and artifacts from various regions and cultures across the continent. The exhibits provide insight into the traditions, beliefs, and creativity of African societies. You'll have the opportunity to learn about African art's historical and cultural significance.

A visit to the Museum of African Arts typically takes around 1.5 to 2 hours, allowing you to immerse yourself in the diverse and captivating exhibits.

The museum is closed on Mondays, so plan your visit accordingly.

Photography may be restricted in some areas, so please follow any guidelines provided by the museum staff.

The museum's gift shop offers a selection of books, crafts, and souvenirs related to African culture and art.

The Museum of African Arts is a culturally enriching experience that allows you to explore the artistic traditions of Africa without leaving Belgrade. Whether you're an art enthusiast, a traveler with a passion for culture, or someone looking to broaden their horizons, this museum offers a unique and insightful journey through the artistic tapestry of Africa.

17. Belgrade City Library

The Belgrade City Library, or Gradska biblioteka Beograd in Serbian, is a cultural hub where literature, knowledge, and history converge. This institution serves as a repository of countless stories and a haven for bibliophiles, offering visitors an enriching experience in the world of books.

The Belgrade City Library is conveniently located in the city center, near the Republic Square and the National Museum. You can easily reach it on foot or by using public transportation, including bus lines 24, 26, 37, or 44. The address is Kosančićev venac 7, Belgrade 11000, Serbia.

Entrance to the Belgrade City Library is typically free of charge. Visitors are welcome to explore the library's resources, reading rooms, and exhibitions without any cost.

Immerse yourself in the library's serene ambiance as you peruse its vast collection of books, periodicals, and cultural resources. The library often hosts exhibitions, lectures, and cultural events, so check for any current offerings during your visit. You can also enjoy quiet reading spaces or simply appreciate the architectural beauty of the building.

The amount of time spent at the Belgrade City Library can vary based on your interests and activities. A typical visit may range from 1 to 2 hours, allowing time for exploration and contemplation.

The library is closed on Sundays, so plan your visit accordingly.

Remember to maintain a peaceful atmosphere in the library, as it is a place for quiet study and reflection.

The Belgrade City Library is a haven for literary enthusiasts and seekers of knowledge. Whether you're an avid reader, a student, or simply someone who appreciates the tranquility of libraries, this institution offers a serene retreat in the heart of Belgrade, where you can explore the world of literature and culture at your own pace.

18. Topčider Park

Topčider Park, or Topčiderski park in Serbian, is a green oasis in the heart of Belgrade, offering a serene respite from the urban hustle and bustle. This historic park is known for its lush landscapes, charming architecture, and a glimpse into the city's past.

Topčider Park is located approximately 4 kilometers from the city center. You can reach it by taxi, public transportation, or on foot. Bus lines 34, 36, and 49, as well as tram line 3, serve the area. The address is Bulevar patrijarha Pavla 1, Belgrade 11050, Serbia.

Entrance to Topčider Park is typically free. Visitors can explore the park's gardens, ponds, and historical sites without any cost.

Wander through the park's winding paths and enjoy the tranquility of nature. Topčider Park is home to several historical landmarks, including the Topčider Palace, the Residence of Prince Miloš, and the Saint Gabriel Monastery. You can also have a relaxing picnic, visit the nearby Topčider Cemetery with its historic tombstones, or simply soak in the park's serene ambiance.

The duration of your visit to Topčider Park can vary based on your interests and activities. A leisurely visit to explore the park and its historical sites may take 2 to 3 hours.

The park is an ideal destination for a peaceful walk, so consider wearing comfortable shoes.

Bring some snacks or a picnic if you plan to spend more time in the park.

Topčider Park's historical sites provide an opportunity to learn about Belgrade's past and the lives of its notable residents.

Consider a visit during the spring when the park's greenery is at its most vibrant.

Topčider Park is a tranquil haven where you can escape the urban hustle of Belgrade and connect with nature and history. Whether you're a history enthusiast, a nature lover, or someone seeking a peaceful escape, this park offers an ideal setting for relaxation and exploration.

19. Belgrade Cathedral (Saborna Crkva)

The Belgrade Cathedral, known as Saborna Crkva in Serbian, is a magnificent Serbian Orthodox church that stands as an architectural masterpiece in the heart of Belgrade. It combines spiritual significance with stunning architectural beauty, making it a must-visit destination for both locals and tourists.

The Belgrade Cathedral is centrally located in the city's historical district, near Knez Mihailova Street and the Republic Square. You can easily reach it on foot, by taxi, or using public transportation. Bus lines 24, 26, and 37, as well as tram line 2, serve the area. The address is Kneza Sime Markovića 5, Belgrade 11000, Serbia.

Entrance to the Belgrade Cathedral is typically free. Visitors are welcome to explore the church's interior, including its stunning frescoes and religious artifacts, without any cost.

Step inside the Belgrade Cathedral to admire its breathtaking interior, featuring intricate frescoes, beautifully adorned iconostasis, and an atmosphere of profound serenity. Take time for quiet reflection, light a candle, and absorb the spiritual ambiance. Additionally, the church often hosts religious ceremonies and events, which you can attend if interested.

A visit to the Belgrade Cathedral usually takes around 30 minutes to an hour, allowing you to appreciate the interior, engage in contemplation, and observe any ongoing ceremonies.

Keep in mind that the church may be closed during certain hours, especially during religious services or ceremonies.

Photography may be restricted inside the church, so please respect any guidelines provided by church staff.

The Belgrade Cathedral, with its exquisite architecture and spiritual depth, provides a peaceful and culturally enriching experience. Whether you're a religious traveler, an architecture enthusiast, or someone seeking a tranquil moment in the heart of Belgrade, this church offers a serene and spiritually resonant visit.

20. Museum of Vuk and Dositej

The Museum of Vuk and Dositej, located in the heart of Belgrade, is a cultural institution that honors the legacy of two prominent figures in Serbian history and language: Vuk Stefanović Karadžić and Dositej Obradović. This museum provides an insightful journey into the development of the Serbian language and its cultural significance.

The museum is conveniently situated in central Belgrade, near Knez Mihailova Street and the Republic Square. You can reach it easily on foot, by taxi, or via public transportation. Bus lines 24, 26, and 37, as well as tram line 2, serve the area. The address is Gospodar Jevremova 21, Belgrade 11000, Serbia.

The approximate ticket price for adults is around 300 Serbian dinars, with reduced fees for students, children, and seniors. The museum is known for its affordability, making it accessible to a wide range of visitors.

Explore the museum's collection, which includes artifacts, documents, and personal belongings of Vuk Stefanović Karadžić and Dositej Obradović. Learn about their contributions to Serbian language reform and literature. The museum often hosts exhibitions, lectures, and cultural events, so be sure to check for any ongoing programs during your visit.

A visit to the Museum of Vuk and Dositej typically takes around 1 to 1.5 hours, providing ample time to engage with the exhibits and immerse yourself in the cultural and historical context.

Photography inside the museum may be restricted, so please respect any guidelines provided by the museum staff.

The museum's location in the historic district offers opportunities for exploring nearby attractions and enjoying a pleasant stroll along Knez Mihailova Street.

The Museum of Vuk and Dositej is a cultural gem that delves into the linguistic and literary heritage of Serbia. Whether you're a language enthusiast, a history buff, or simply someone interested in exploring Serbian culture, this museum offers a unique and insightful journey into the lives and contributions of Vuk and Dositej.

21. Zemun Old Town

Zemun Old Town, located on the banks of the Danube River, is a picturesque district with a rich history and a unique charm. This well-preserved area boasts a distinct architectural and cultural heritage, making it a delightful destination for travelers seeking to explore Belgrade's past.

Zemun Old Town is easily accessible from the city center by public transportation or taxi. Bus lines 15, 84, and 704, as well as tram line 2, connect the city center to Zemun. The journey typically takes around 30 minutes. If you prefer a scenic route, you can also take a boat ride along the Danube to reach Zemun.

Exploring Zemun Old Town is free of charge. Visitors can stroll through the historic streets, enjoy the views of the Danube, and soak in the local atmosphere without any cost.

Wander through the charming streets of Zemun Old Town, admiring its well-preserved architecture, including colorful houses and historic landmarks like the Gardoš Tower. Visit the Madlenianum Opera and Theatre, or simply relax at one of the many riverside cafes while enjoying the panoramic views of the Danube. Don't miss the historic Zemun Quay, a promenade lined with restaurants and bars where you can savor Serbian cuisine.

Exploring Zemun Old Town can take several hours to a full day, depending on your interests. A leisurely stroll through the historic streets, a visit to the Gardoš Tower, and a meal at one of the local eateries can easily fill an enjoyable day.

The Gardoš Tower offers panoramic views of Zemun and the Danube River. Consider climbing to the top for stunning photo opportunities.

Zemun is known for its relaxed and laid-back atmosphere. It's an ideal place to unwind and enjoy the slower pace of life.

Zemun Old Town provides a captivating journey into the past and an opportunity to enjoy the tranquil Danube riverside. Whether you're a history enthusiast, a food lover, or someone seeking a leisurely day of exploration, Zemun Old Town offers a delightful escape from the urban buzz of Belgrade.

When visiting Belgrade here are 7 valuable pieces of advice to keep in mind:

1. Respect Local Customs: Be mindful of Serbian customs and traditions. When visiting religious sites or churches, dress modestly, covering your shoulders and knees. It's also customary to greet people with a handshake and say "Dobar dan" (Good day) when entering a room.

2. Currency and Payments: The official currency is the Serbian dinar. While credit cards are widely accepted in urban areas, it's advisable to carry some cash, especially when visiting smaller establishments or local markets.

3. Language: While many people in Belgrade, especially in the service industry, speak English, it's polite to learn a few basic Serbian phrases. Locals appreciate when tourists make an effort to communicate in the local language.

4. Public Transportation: Belgrade has an efficient and cost-effective public transportation system, including buses and trams. Purchase tickets in advance or use contactless payment methods. Taxis are also readily available, but make sure they use a meter.

5. Safety: Belgrade is generally a safe city for tourists. However, exercise the same precautions you would in any major city, like safeguarding your belongings and avoiding poorly lit areas at night.

6. Local Cuisine: Serbian cuisine is diverse and delicious. Don't miss trying traditional dishes like ćevapi (grilled minced meat), sarma (cabbage rolls), and local wines and rakija (fruit brandy).

7. Social Scene: Belgrade is known for its vibrant nightlife. The city comes alive after dark, with numerous clubs, bars, and restaurants staying open late. If you plan to experience the nightlife, dress appropriately and be prepared for energetic crowds.

By following these tips, you'll be well-prepared to explore Belgrade, immerse yourself in its culture, and enjoy a safe and memorable visit to this dynamic city.

Here are 7 of the best services to consider using:

1. Belgrade Tourist Info Centers: These centers offer maps, brochures, and expert advice on what to see and do in the city. They can help you plan your itinerary and provide information on local events and attractions.

2. Public Transportation: Belgrade's public transportation system is convenient and affordable. Consider using buses and trams to explore the city easily. You can purchase single tickets or daily passes for access to the entire network.

3. Taxi Services: Taxis are readily available in Belgrade. Look for reputable taxi companies and make sure the driver uses a meter or agrees on a fare before starting the ride. Uber and other ride-sharing apps are also options.

4. Accommodation Booking Websites: Use platforms like Booking.com, Airbnb, or local hotel websites to find accommodations that suit your preferences and budget. Many Belgrade hosts and hotels offer excellent service and value.

5. Guided Tours: Joining guided tours, whether walking, bus, or boat tours, is a great way to gain insights into Belgrade's history, culture, and attractions. Local guides can provide in-depth knowledge and make your visit more educational.

6. Language Translation Apps: Download translation apps to assist with communication, especially if you don't speak Serbian. Apps like Google Translate can be handy for quick translations and basic conversations.

7. Restaurant and Food Delivery Apps: Belgrade offers a rich culinary scene. Use food delivery apps like Glovo, Wolt, or Donesi.com to enjoy local dishes and international cuisine from the comfort of your accommodation.

By utilizing these services, you can navigate Belgrade with ease, access valuable information, and make the most of your visit to this vibrant and historic city.

Top 7 Must-Try Dining Spots in Belgrade:

1. Skadarlija Restaurants: Skadarlija is Belgrade's historic Bohemian Quarter, known for its cobblestone streets and traditional Serbian restaurants. Enjoy live music, local dishes like ćevapi and sarma, and a lively atmosphere at restaurants like Tri Šešira and Dva Jelena.

2. Question Mark (Znak pitanja): Located in the city center, this historic restaurant offers a unique dining experience in an 19th-century building with a "?" sign. Try Serbian and international dishes in a charming, old-world setting.

3. Ambar: Situated on the banks of the Sava River, Ambar offers a modern take on Balkan cuisine. Enjoy a selection of mezze, grilled dishes, and Balkan wines while taking in beautiful river views.

4. Iguana: For a taste of international cuisine, visit Iguana. This trendy restaurant serves a variety of dishes, from sushi to steak, and offers a bustling atmosphere perfect for a night out.

5. Manufaktura: Located in a historic building in the Dorćol district, Manufaktura offers a menu that combines traditional Serbian flavors with modern culinary techniques. The ambiance and presentation are as impressive as the food.

6. Homa Bistrot: A hidden gem in the city, Homa Bistrot offers a fusion of European and Serbian cuisine. It's known for its innovative dishes, friendly staff, and cozy atmosphere.

7. Idiot Bar: If you're looking for a quirky and fun dining experience, Idiot Bar is the place to go. The menu features creative and playful dishes, and the eclectic décor adds to the unique atmosphere.

These dining spots represent just a taste of the diverse culinary offerings in Belgrade. Whether you're seeking traditional Serbian dishes or international flavors, you're sure to find a dining experience to suit your palate.

Here are 7 crucial phone numbers to know:

1. Emergency Services (Police, Fire, Ambulance): For immediate help in case of an emergency, dial **112**. This number connects you to the appropriate emergency service, whether it's the police, fire department, or ambulance.

2. Medical Assistance: To reach medical assistance, call **194**. This number connects you to the nearest healthcare facility and emergency medical services.

3. Belgrade City Information: If you have general inquiries or need assistance related to the city, call the Belgrade City Information Center at **+381 11 292 1212**. They can provide information about public services, transportation, and more.

4. Tourist Police: For non-emergency assistance or to report minor incidents involving tourists, you can contact the Tourist Police at **+381 62 8245 072.**

5. Lost or Stolen Credit Cards: If you lose your credit card or it's stolen, contact your bank immediately. It's essential to have your bank's contact number or the international card services number readily available.

6. Embassies and Consulates: It's a good idea to have the contact information for your country's embassy or consulate in Belgrade in case you encounter any issues or emergencies related to your citizenship while in Serbia.

7. Taxi Services: Save the contact information for a reputable taxi company in Belgrade. Some well-known taxi services include Pink Taxi **(+381 11 9801)** and Naxis Taxi **(+381 11 30 555 55).**

Having these phone numbers on hand ensures you're prepared for various situations during your stay in Belgrade, from emergencies to general inquiries and assistance.

7 unknown facts about Belgrade:

1. Intersection of Two Rivers: Belgrade is one of the few major European cities located at the confluence of two major rivers—the Sava and the Danube. This unique geographical position has influenced the city's history and culture.

2. A City of Many Names: Over the centuries, Belgrade has had many names. One of its historical names, Singidunum, dates back to Roman times. Throughout its history, it has been called Alba Graeca, Nándorfehérvár, and Beograd, among others.

3. Belgrade's Unique Military History: The city has been the site of more than 115 wars and battles over its history. It has been destroyed and rebuilt numerous times, making it a resilient symbol of Serbia's spirit.

4. Inventor Nikola Tesla's Hometown: The famous inventor Nikola Tesla, known for his contributions to electricity and engineering, was born in the village of Smiljan in modern-day Croatia but identified himself as an ethnic Serb. He spent part of his early life in Belgrade.

5. Belgrade's Underground Tunnels: Beneath the streets of Belgrade lies an extensive network of underground tunnels, some of which were used during World War II and the Cold War. These tunnels are not widely known or accessible to the public.

6. Kalemegdan: A Park and Fortress in One: Kalemegdan Park is not just a beautiful park with panoramic views; it's also home to the historic Kalemegdan Fortress. The name "Kalemegdan" is of Turkish origin and means "battlefield fortress."

7. A Vibrant Nightlife: Belgrade is known for its lively nightlife, but what's lesser-known is the city's thriving floating clubs, or "splavovi," which are situated on the riverbanks of the Sava and Danube rivers. These clubs offer a unique party experience with music, drinks, and scenic river views.

These lesser-known facts add depth and intrigue to Belgrade's already captivating history and culture. The city's rich past, unique geography, and vibrant atmosphere make it a fascinating destination for travelers.

Printed in Great Britain
by Amazon